w/c
＋ 1.50

LIONHEARTED™

The closer I get,
the more I see
how far I am.
Rumi

www.lionhearted.org.uk

The Emperor's New Self

Finding Certainty

Andrew D Harry

The Emperor's New Self
by Andrew D Harry

First published in 2018
by Andrew D Harry

A catalogue card for this book is available from the British Library.

Paperback ISBN: 978-1-9164951-9-7
Hardback ISBN: 978-1-9164951-0-4
Ebook ISBN: 978-1-9164951-2-8

Front cover from the original drawing of "The Esencia Model" by
Andrew D Harry copyright © June 2016 www.esencia.org.uk as presented
now by graphic designer Barnaby Attwell.

Front page illustration "Lionhearted" adapted under licence from
copyright © October 2015 by Epitanbev via Shutterstock Image ID
187844723

Printed and bound in Great Britain by
TJ International, Padstow, Cornwall

Dedication

I dedicate this book to my children, Samuel, Alice and Robyn, to my fabulous wife Joy and my friends and family worldwide. To my parents Mary and Dennis who set the conditions for my maturation. Thank you all for your love and support.

Acknowledgements

I would like to acknowledge everyone who has met me on my journey and helped me along the way. Whether you know it or not, your contribution has been invaluable. I am certain you know who you are. Thank you to Ivor and Elizabeth Perry for your support so long ago and to Marcus Wyn Robinson, a very special spirit. To Graham and Lyn Whiteman who have demonstrated such courage in forging a new path into a paradigm that is so old it now appears new. I am honoured to have been able to collaborate in this great endeavour and am privileged in continuing to do so. These are challenging times and yet also exciting. I look ahead and welcome a host of new folk crossing my path and enriching my life, as I seek to enrich theirs.

Forward

A re-framing of the nature and definition of relaxation, as a vital element of exploring the nature of the conscious self and how to directly experience it. I sincerely hope you enjoy this little book and benefit from it as intended. So, relax deeply, feel better and enjoy your life more.

Introduction

This book was conceived some nine years ago in an attempt to provide the reader/listener with a direct experience of the therapeutic process that leads to better health and well-being. It is a distillation of the process and lessons I have learnt that have helped me towards fulfilling my wish of finding certainty. There have been surprises along the way and the insights won have been captured and conveyed with as much clarity as possible, to reflect what has been defined as a personal revolution through relaxation. A revolution that leads to the realization of potential. It is a truly soulful rebellion.

Andrew D Harry
Penzance,
Cornwall
2018

Contents

Winter Sun

Winter sun slants off the water
into my eyes.
Seagull cries
overhead.
I sit on this bench alone,
miles from home,
knowing
I could be with you
instead,
but
I am
sitting here
on my own,
enslaved to the man,
feeling like an also-ran
in the great scheme of life.

There must be more than this
strife.

Day in day out,
I doubt
they would hear me shout
even at the top of my voice.

But,
who are they to me?

We shall see.
Moving on then to more of the same,
day in, day out,
again and again.

There must be more than this.

No way out.
They wouldn't even hear me shout.

I don't even know what I'd have to say.

Oh well,
here's to the end
of another day.
I guess this is just how it is,
but I can't help thinking,
that there must be
more to it all
than this.

Incessant Fear

Disconnected.
Out of reach.
The beauty that I see
would still go on
if I were gone.
It's just that it wouldn't be seen,
by me.

Life goes on
relentlessly.
Year on year.
more life to be ended.
Worn out by an incessant fear,
so harsh
that if all there is to this
is blood and sweat
and worms,
it is hardly a heart-warming thought.
Should it be for nought?

All this toil and effort,
what's it for?
Going back to the earth
to sustain more?

More of the same uncaring life.
If I am good
in a way they have defined,
I will have achieved,
a life refined,
but if the refinement of all this loss is loss,
I can't find a crumb of hope in it,
just dross.

Toil and effort
to carve out this life.
More work and more toil,
until I merge with the soil,
to spread me even thinner.
Even the worms that feast on me
will be eaten by birds,
and the birds in turn will end up
as something else's dinner.

Instead of dreams of more grind,
my goal is
to rise above this,
to find
a place to soothe my soul.

Wherever that is.
Perhaps even
away from this life
that is so unkind.

Why would I put myself through
more of the same,
again and again?
Through cycles of gloom,
impending,
never ending,
doom.

I might as well be kind
to myself at least
and end it all.
Not in the vain hope of achieving some peace,
but to be released
and no longer suffer
this shit.

I wouldn't know then
if it were to carry on
without me,
but the pain and my loss
and this shit,
would be gone.

Eat Drink Work Sleep

I am going to do something
about this.
I am fed up
with this lonely, daily grind.

In order to put my plan together
I will need to find
some time
but I haven't even got the time to think
just eat
and drink
and work
and sleep.

I am beginning to act like a sheep.
Baa baa.
Blah blah.
Yes Sir,
No Sir,
Three bags full Sir.

Back in the groove,
not able to move.
Whirr,
fizz,

bleep.
The machine goes on
and on
and on
and on.

Slowly, suddenly,
once again,
all ideas of hope
are gone.
Gone.

Back in the groove,
not able to move.
Whirr, fizz, bleep.
Eat, drink, work, sleep.
My own ideas in full retreat.
Whirr, fizz, bleep.
Eat, drink, work, sleep.

Arrogance

Is it arrogance sublime
that I have
given so much of my time
and attention
to automatic reaction,
unwanted distraction,
now beyond its prime?

In giving credence
to those thoughts unseen,
I have allowed my fears
to rule the roost,
unchallenged,
unfettered,
my faults assumed,
dominating.
I have been paralysed,
consumed.

What possible, credible purpose is being served,
in behaving as I do?
If only I knew
how to change the script.

Just what can I do

to help me climb out
of this self-imposed crypt
and leave this zoo.

I am
slowly, cautiously, painfully,
becoming aware
of this log in my eye
that so limits my view.

If only I knew
how to move it aside,
I would no longer have to hide
behind automatic responses
designed to protect,
but now only resulting in neglect
of those I love
and who love me too.

I have just got to get out of this zoo.

Piece by piece
I will unravel
this web
that so grieves my heart
and confounds my head.

I have decided
that the only thing left

to do right now
is work out how
to start.

I haven't a clue
what to do,
nor even how to begin.

After all,
what do I know,
mere mortal that I am?
As I sit here
in this wretched state,
wanting to know love,
anticipating only hate.

Pathetic,
wretched,
all alone.
Racked with more of the same
pain and shame.
My only friend is my deep,
unavoidable, cleansing grief.
It has not yet offered me even a crumb of relief.

All my hope is gone.
What to do,
to get out of this zoo?
I wish I knew.

Change

Change.
Such a perplexing word.
Change, exactly what?

I really do not know,
but, if I do not change
I will remain the same.
Remain the same,
the same as what?

It is misery
that is prevailing.
My soul is failing.
Failing in this wretched state,
that I am beginning to hate.

Round and round and
round and round.
Wretched, loss prevailing.
Fears, anxieties assailing.

Everyone else tells me what to do,
to think and do and be.

They tell me

how I must act
in order to succeed.

To be successful
in this life,
so fruitless.
A chore.

Why,
would I
want to succeed
more,
at satisfying a hidden man's need?

Just because he or she can shout
and drown everyone else out.
Telling me what to think,
to eat,
to drink,
to love,
and hate.
How did I get in this awful state?

This state where I do as the hidden man pleases.
"Do as he says and you will be fine.
You will have what you want
and be free of diseases."
To work some more and ruin my health,
at least I will be on the road to wealth.

Lining someone else's pockets,
while surviving,
when I could be thriving,
a-living.

Sitting here writing and reflecting
on this dross,
all I can feel is a sense of loss.

Which doesn't tie in with what I have been told.

"Work hard,
do as we say,
and the streets will be paved with gold."

Spend all my time
focussing on someone else's definition
of success
and I will have all that I want,
but instead I get less!

Though if what I want
is defined by another,
whose wants keep changing,
why bother?

As soon as I reach the next level
there's another and another,

that wasn't apparent before.

Another door.

Still,
a few more strides
and I'll be there.

At a place that is always being redefined,
that routinely perplexes
my mind
and is
always
just
out of reach.

Fractured Narrative

Forget what the man says.

What is it I really want?

I don't know where to start.

I've hardly even given it a moment's thought,
as the man has had all my attention,
my effort,
my sinews,
my heart.

I suppose what I really want
is to know
what is it that I need?

Well that's a beginning,
a seed.

If ever so tenuous,
but why not?

Everything else
is becoming so
bloody strenuous.

I need
to sleep-in and rest.
Get things off my chest.
Take some time
to define,
what is important
to me
and what it is I believe.

What have I learned from this
so far?

Well, I have listened to everyone else for a start.

From now on,
I think
I will take heed of myself
and my heart.

There is night and day,
black and white,
up and down,
dark and light.
I wake and sleep,
may live and die.
There is in and out,
below and above.
There is loss and gain.

There is hate and love.
There is hot and cold.
Having an opinion
and being told.
There is empty and full.
There is high and low.
There is hard and soft,
and Sun and Moon,
future and past,
too late and too soon.

It seems to me
that in the world,
that I can see,
there are always two sides to each story.

So, why is it that the prevailing view
presents only one side as the road to glory?

If the man says this is right
it's surely quite possible
that what he says is shite?

It is,
after all,
only one side of the picture...

Interesting thought?

So, at this juncture,
I will certainly
have to explore,
this,
a little more.

A Different Road

Turned down a different road[1] today,
on my way to lunch.

Everything seemed so clear.
My head full of new ideas.

I even acted on a hunch.

I was fitful over the meeting at two
and was frightened
at what I thought
others might do.

Then over a tasty chicken soup,
I stepped beyond my usual loop,
of habitual reactions
and emotional distractions,
and realised
it was my thoughts of
what others might do
that were tying me in knots.

So frightened of
my own projections,
of fears,

of habitually anticipated,
future rejections.

Now
it is time
to stop
associating certainty with fear
and instead begin to doubt
the fear itself
when it sticks its head out.

I choose to be certain instead,
of something,
of anything else,
but not for once
the commanding,
demanding,
ever expanding,
fears in my head.

I have been so overwhelmed,
by this dominance of fear,
that it has begun
to become abundantly clear
that what I think I hear,
this sound
of the pounding
of dread,
is not really real

at all,
it's all
in my
head.

So,
at long last
I am going to choose
to break the spell
I have cast
and choose
to be
certain instead.

Certain?
Certain of what?
Well, certain of anything but
that fear in my head.

Getting Out Of The Zoo

I want to change the way I feel.

Now!

Not in some hazy, distant moment
but I have always thought that
I don't know how.

Is somebody else somehow responsible for this
or is the solution waiting, hidden within me?

What if I stopped going out
and instead went more fully in?

Will the echoes of my wounds
still chill my soul,
or could they quietly,
gently start to sing
another tune?

Some help[2]
as my efforts converge
assists the free flow
of energy,
provides a breakthrough, brings clarity.

Connections appear, obviously.

Is this an ancient opportunity?

Am I free to simply create a choice,
as I find the courage
to know what is my truth?

And end my dependence on another's view?

With compassion for myself
I can now choose
to tread my own path.

After what has seemed such a long time,
residing under the yoke of another man's
dreams
it seems
that I am beginning to believe
that I am ready,
to choose to exercise my power,
through action
and expression
in each moment.
In repeating this process
I have begun to begin
to recognise my true nature,
and see that now in others too.

Have I found
a promising door-way
that may help lead me out of this zoo?

By knowing what it is
I want
I am beginning to be
transformed and able,
to choose to transform more.
On an endless cycle
revolving and evolving,
becoming,
grounded and certain.

It is my right!

So, quickly
and effortlessly,
I surprise myself in my ability
to be more fully me.

As if for the first time
a concept of safety
begins to appear.

Yet,
it becomes clear,
it has been

and is
always
here
and now,
above and below,
within and without.

There is no need to suffer more
any lingering trace of doubt.

As I start to take
my first, final,
faltering steps
on my road to becoming whole,
I need not now assume
that the road is arduous and long,
but can entertain the thought
that I might just have been delightfully wrong!

With patience and attention
I have noticed
my rigid, inner shadows
start to move.

I am manifesting wholeness
In what can only be termed an
embodiment
of self-love.

First ascending then descending
I know now
that love is here to stay.
It cannot go away.

Though apparently fleeting,
it is kindled and remains eternal.

I have embraced it.
For I know that
there is no need to chase it.

For it is already
impatiently
chasing
me.

What A Day

Well, well,
what a day.

What is this I say?

"I couldn't possibly,
definitely not!"
but yes
these chains are released
and out these fears trot.

What to do with them
when they reveal
the opportunity
for myself
to heal?

I can choose
to take hold of them
and turn them around.

Initially this sounds
clumsy out of sync,
yet, each time I notice
I can stop

and drink them in
until they begin
to sing
another tune.

I can follow each thread
wherever it may lead,
to new expressions,
unseen needs.

Gradually I can
begin to feel
the opposite of each
could well be real.

What then,
I ask,
as I start to flow[3],
what do I want?

Only I can know.

Only I can know,
what it is I want
to say
or do,

to act[4]
and express myself,

as I take a step along a brave
new
road.

I can cast aside ideals
imposed by others
I have held in positions of misplaced authority.

They cannot feel what
I can feel,
nor know
what it is
I need.

I must trust myself now.
I am unique
and maybe
the universe relies on the dreams I seed.

I must seed those dreams and nurture them well
and release myself from the bonds
that hold me back.

I have no need to doubt,
any more,
but can choose to be,
certain,
for sure.

To be bold,
I need merely hold
my attention on what
I choose.
What it is I want to feel[5]
and choose to feel it again
and again and again.

And as my doubts retreat,
slowly and inexorably
I sense what it is
to be
certain.

I can after all know
what it is I need,
I have,
I want,
I feel,
I am.

Each time
I take stock
and know
that even though
each seems a tiny step
towards a distant star,
in no time at all
the mighty bounds

they become
reveal that I
have
travelled
far.

Even to
the growing edge[6]
of the Universe
and back.

To share what I have learned.

To coax, cajole
another soul,
to know they too won't get burned.

When they leave the surface of their moon
and like me
plunge into the depths
of their sun.

The Veil

Awareness can surely be seen
as the screen[7]
on which
all my thoughts and ideas
are projected?

So, what is the source
of this screen,
that so intimately
observes all the facets
of my life,
yet sits there undetected?

Instead of waiting lifetimes then
to discover what lies
beyond
the sand,
sea
and sky,
I can surely
first try
to seek
to find
this screen
that lies

unseen
behind
the apparent
labyrinth
of
my
mind?
It seems to me
that this obscure horizon could be
the very source of my being?

Now,
that would certainly be
exceedingly
freeing,
if true!

Becoming Whole

Along the road to becoming whole,
lies the building of
the diamond soul.

Mist hangs thick and cool.
As the sun's rays elicit warmth
for the new day.

Rivulets of myth and bliss
flow along the growing edge
of the
new dawn
as
rose and lily,
on window ledge,
scent the air.
Light streams on dreams and industry.

A knowing smile breaks out
on all who enter the establishment
of presence.

It is a place to ground
and truly
connect

to this hectic world
of black and white
and the illusion
of what's wrong
and
to what's
right.

To fuse with love
another way
and balance impulse
gone astray,
to clear the path to harmony.

What I need
is what I feel,
It is what I want
and have.

I am the link to parity
and a simple law of love.

Now is the time to be myself
and to move
with clarity.

To build upon
foundations tested
through gracious hearts

and loving hands
I have
rested.

No longer whether,
but now when,
without as within,
the time is nigh.

My feet in the earth
and my head in the sky.

I am in my element.

A home at last
now I am able,
to express and to involve,
to bustle and hustle
and take my place
to nourish from
my table.

Without compromise or dilution,
I will act
on my own
terms.

I'll take no truck
and pass

no buck
for there
is
work
to do.

Until subject and object
are one,
when the race
will have been
run
up the mountain of the Moon,
on our journey
to the Sun.

My place can be found
in the building
of the diamond soul.
that lies along
the road
to becoming
whole.

Claim Your Peace

In your whole life
have you ever known
a moment
without fear?

Well,
draw near,
for I have a tale to tell.

It may well
come as some surprise
but the mechanical mind
cannot reprise
the solution,
but will certainly
continue
to deliver
ever more
light
pollution.

Let it do its job,
it is not here to rob
your soul,
but

to help you achieve
your goal.

There is however,
no point waiting
for the conflict to cease,
to win this war
you must
first
claim
your
peace[8].

Close To Home

My well-practised need
to control,
born of anxiety
and fear,
has led me to
here.

To this place
of trouble
that always seems
to double
when even now
I often try
harder
to
control
what I see
or what I think
is happening
to me.

I have unintentionally
gone
to some extraordinary lengths
that test

my strengths
to endure physical, emotional
and spiritual pain,
without a jot
of apparent
gain.

This clever cul-de-sac
has been
like an existential
trap.

Yet here
in this other intimate place
the less
I try to control
the more certain I become
and the closer I am
to home.
I am blessed.

New Beginning

Enough of this!
I know there is more.

I know it at my very core.

What it is I want to find,
lies beyond
the fractured screen
of my mind.

It is the certain
ground of being
that lies beyond
the dimmed
and intoxicating
veil of my seeing.

I choose now
to change
the way I deal
with my life,
again.

The very nature of my mind to polarise
is relentlessly

and ruthlessly
exploited
by rabid corporations
and ambitious
men.

It is through
an over reliance on thought
that I have wrought,
the equivalence
of
nought.

An apparent
phantom of phenomena
that so distracts and conceals
and that forges
a tempting,
endless path
to my mind
so apparently
real,
but I now must remember
once again,
how to feel.

A new beginning,
gently,
warmly, softly

deep
within
my heart.

Let me be clear,
there is neither
nostalgia
nor
effort here.

In feeling,
I can simply
find my way
and make
a fresh new
certain
start.

In every moment
of every day,
this tinge of certainty
surprisingly,
begins
to hold
sway.

It is now assuredly,
abundantly
clear to me

that I can only truly feel
for certain
what it is
to be
real,
when
I feel
it in the neglected chambers
of my heart.

The effort of retreating
to the veil behind my mind,
can now
be left
behind,
as it laboriously
continues
its computational task.

A probable simulation,
likely designed
to compare and contrast
on its arduous, unending,
ultimately disappointing
and limiting quest[9].

The illusion of
the Emperor's new Self,
this awareness of awareness,

can now
assuredly
be carefully
placed
on the tool-shed's shelf.

Alternatively now,
I can embark on a journey
so potent and profound,
and in clarence[10] conjure a feeling akin to the
warmth
from a curled up, drowsy kitten,
nestled comfortable
and safe,
purring
upon my
breast.

Wherein my simmering,
true potential,
my very soul,
can
reliably,
quietly,
certainly,
simply
be
found,

beyond the maelstrom
of my mind,
where it has lain
patiently
waiting for me,
deep within
the comfort
of my chest.

The Kitten Stirs

Despite
the mind's
relentless contrast
and distraction
my attention
has settled
on a centre,
of unequalled
precision.

Where a certainty of self,
I feel,
resides
and replaces the mind's
disappointing and fractured
though
very useful
vision.

As if emerging
from a mystical haze,
I am now immune
from the Medusa's
gaze.

With ease embedded,
I know with certainty,
exactly,
where my attention
is headed.

I am
free to move
through a ever clearing lens
of deepening love.

As silk flows over steel
there is no need to resist
but to simply feel
my rested best[11].

I know
what it is now
to truly,
certainly,
be real,
to exist.

As I feel it,
I then choose
to feel it,
even more.

Slowly,
deftly,
subtly,
it delivers
a deeper,
altogether
different,
though
essentially,
familiar
shore.

I can swim to it,
I can dive right in.

Effortlessly
falling,
I fall
into it
again
some more.

I have now found
solid and certain
ground
for sure.

Transformed,
the once vaguely sensed,

dozing feline
is now stirring
from its mythical slumber,
unfurling,
maturing
and confidently realizing
a leonine-like roar.

As I choose
to feel it,
I can choose
to feel it
even more
and more
and more
with certainty,
ever deeper,
fractally,
repeatedly,
to my
very
core.
Then every day,
in every way,
I am
a mere choice
of letting go
away.

I relish the opportunity
to learn
to relax
more deeply
until
once again
I reach
that certain,
content-free point
where heart and soul
are definitely,
eternally,
understood,
for good.

Without constraint
I free fall within
and then
I free fall some more
into it again
and again
and again.
I am certain
and then
I am certain
even more.

Each time
more focussed

yet less
intense.

Each time
I lose myself
I find myself
more.

Each time
as I feel
there is
less pretence.

Each time
re-defining,
with a crystalline certainty
in my
core.

Each time
less alone
and more at home.

A life
now re-born.

A new beginning.

With each cycle

I know
I am winning,
the race to the centre
to my rested best,
my very
self.

At the centre
and
at the growing edge
of all
I stand
apart,
consciously grounded
in my
heart.

The Cosmic Seed

My mind, though wide awake,
and now aware of itself,
is left reeling,
when I realize
that I have been unaware that
*you can't think
a feeling*®12.

Feeling,
with such depth
and scope
lies beyond
the mindful
dichotomy
of fear
and hope,
and the futility
of effort and strife
and opens me
to the whole
where I find
resides
my soul.

The very purpose

of my life.

So, relax
and know
that
you too
can create
the conditions to make
a simple choice,
to either
think or feel.
A simple,
yet apparently
difficult decision,
to truly,
eternally,
certainly
be
real.

It has
no volition,
no conditions,
no opinions,
no grievance,
no difference,
no preference,
no hope
no fear

no now
no here.

So relax,
feel better
and enjoy life
more.

Refresh yourself,
drink it in.

It's easier than
you think!

In this conscious awareness
find the order
that leads
to the source
of your essence,
the cosmic
seed.

Beyond Belief

My mind
wide awake
and merely aware of itself
is now reeling
when I realize
that
consciousness
is not a thought,
but a feeling!

All my life
It seemed to me
that the world is imposed
by what I sense and see.

With no other way
apparent to me
I have chosen
to merely
be aware
of all that
I think and sense and see.

In believing in what I see
and sense and think as well,

this little wooden toy
who within
has been
devoid
of any sense
of joy,
has programmed,
woven even,
its own personal spell,
and alone
has created
a unique
kind of hell.

I have meticulously
refined
my own magic potion,
to suffer and to ensure
that I have remained
a mere drop
in the ocean.

Frightened,
out of balance
and uncertain
I still try so hard
to control,
something,
anything

to find
what I think
will bring me
peace
of mind.

The more I try
to identify
with all I sense
and think
and see
the more
I fall apart.

I only now
ever get it
together
when I simply
feel it
deep within
my heart.

I have tried
and tried
to think myself
out of this place,
but with ever greater effort,
the available space
in my head

gets less
and less
and I
must confess
that the problem
is only ever solved
when I give up
my need
to control
and accept
that
all I need do
is to feel,
to let go.

I am
also moved
to say
that
it has come
as some relief
to find
a simple way
to move
beyond balance
and belief,
to open myself
to the exposure
to confidence

and composure
as I aspire
to dwell
in a certain centre
that has its own
deft pull,
guaranteeing
a feeling
that is
peaceable,
calm and full.

Like comfrey
is nourished
from the earth,
radically,
grow deeply
into your certainty
and know
your worth.

Trying to think
this feeling
is an impossible task.
It is simply madness,
so please
don't ask.

Clarion Call

With circum-punctuality
I stumbled upon
the answer
to a question
I did not think
to ask.

I had unwittingly unmasked,
a folly
of epic proportions,
even now sustaining
mindful
projections and distortions,
that obscure
a powerful truth.
For now,
consciousness and awareness
can be described as
two different things,
according to this
kinaesthetic sleuth.

The latter you will find
sustains a limited view
and perpetual toil in your mind,

the former the feeling
of the proverbial
wind in our wings,
for you to soar above
on beats of love
and directly experience
the certain feeling
where the sky simply
has no ceiling[13].

Know this
and you and your soul
will never again
be apparently parted.

You will have
become
"lion-hearted".

So, let your inner heart-felt roar
well-up and send
a clarion call
far and wide,
to invite
one and all
to join the pride.

That When Now

The poets and sages of old,
belovedly sold,
the notion
THAT
there exists,
a plausible connection,
a way,
to the light.

Where after suitable progress
through introspection
we will have become
heaven blessed
when our mere temporal lives
have ended
and we have
transcended
our baser nature.

When we have become
physically,
emotionally
and spiritually
wise
and have realized

that the ultimate prize
lies at the end
of our very own
path to paradise.

What is offered in this book
is another way to look
at the precise mechanism behind
the journey to transcend
the mechanical
monkey mind
and help you find
what it is you want.

It is not the font
of all knowledge
that is true,
but it will go some way
to reveal
exactly
what is stopping you[14].

Victory

Images from lore
offer a little more
in our quest,
to recover
the optimal state
that is our rested best.

The double-edged sword represents
the fractured narrative
of the mind.

Designed
to compare
and contrast,
to keep us
creatively and fully
engaged
to the present
and the past,
and to stay
vulnerable
to extremes
and perpetually,
shallow

and manipulative
memes.

If instead we embrace
and place our trust
in the fractal nature
of our hearts
as a priority
and in listening passively
we free ourselves
from our self-imposed bondage
of mindful, misguided
and limiting strategies
and in this unfathomable medium
remain safely shielded.

To truly put our armour on,
all we now need do,
is take it off.

Through embodiment[15]
we can now safely
execute our return
from Oz
because
only from the heart,
can you touch
the sky[16].

Know then
that the I
knows HOW
and only you
know WHEN
and there is
no WHY.

But where to start?
Rely not on
the I of the mind,
but on the I of the heart.

The former sustains
perpetual strife,
the latter the gateway
to an eternal
life.

This habitual reliance
on mere thinking
must
STOP.

If you are to become
the divine
ocean
in this simply
human

drop[17].

Before flowing
out,
fully,
you have
the key
to enter in.

Connected thus,
the very Universe
is ours.

Once again
remember that,
only when
the Sun sets
can we see
the Stars.

So, sense it
feel it,
trust it,
love it
and above all
begin
to relax,
no effort
required.

Simply choose
and feel
inspired.

Wu Wei Hsin

It is not absurd to think
that the more certain
of self
I become
the greater
I feel it
in my heart,
that I know and trust
that we are one.

If we faithfully embrace
this simple little rule,
we can all realize
the perfect, pure potential
of
Zero the fool.

References and Notes

1. Inspired by what I recall being a Buddhist teaching called "the 5 Verses" (source: Anon) about walking down a road full of potholes, learning how to climb out of a pothole and avoiding falling into further potholes and then eventually choosing to walk down a different road. Sound advice.

2. Help is at hand from The Relaxation Academy (see www.therelaxationacademy.com).

3. Relating to the renowned "Flow Sequence" developed by Graham and Lyn Whiteman and as described in their book "Stress Less, More Success" published by 10-10-10 Publishing in 2015.

4. Inspired here by the book "Life is Tremendous" by Charles "Tremendous" Jones, wherein the idea is espoused that "whatever you believe, act as if it is true." It challenges each of us to wrestle with the very nature of belief. A great little book, thanks Charles.

5. Here I relate to the monumental publication that is "A Course in Miracles". A book, by Helen Schucman published in 1976, a year-long study of daily affirmations, including the classic "I am responsible for what I see, I choose the feelings I experience and the goals I will achieve." In its exploration of changing the inner narrative, it is a challenging and transformative read.

6. Doctor Randolph Stone, the founder of Polarity Therapy used this term "the growing edge" to define our journey to challenge and push back our boundary conditions. Set out in 2 Volumes The Complete Collected

Works by CLCS Wellness Books, Dr Stone's system is a vast treatise on the ancient modality of Energy Medicine.

7. The Hindu concept of jnana yoga/vichara (self-enquiry) espoused in the book "Be as you are" containing the teachings of Sri Ramana Maharshi edited by David Godman and published by Arkana.

8. Inspired by a conversation in an episode in Series One of Star Trek Discovery, a Netflix Original Series, 2017.

9. Inspired by the book "Krishnamurti and the Unity of Man" by Carlo Suares published in 1982 by Chetana wherein Krishnamurti describes the moment when we become finally and fully disappointed by his mind, and that it is only then can we move on to mature and grow into our true nature. I happened to pluck this small volume from my friend Scott's collection of books that were languishing on my bookshelves when he was lodging on my boat Prydwen in 2015. As often happens I picked up the book, opened it randomly and this little gem of a notion came into focus in front of me on the page. I immediately realized that if we are not to be disappointed perpetually then we must look for certainty elsewhere than the mind. All at once all streams converged, I knew where and how to find certainty and the rest is history. Thank you Scott Thompson, JD Krishnamurti and Graham /Lyn Whiteman for this serendipitous event.

10. The affectionate name for a horse-drawn carriage with a clear glass front. The heir to the British throne is known as "The Clarence" and lives at "Clarence House". At Esencia Relaxation this term has been re-framed. Our re-definition radically reclaims our sovereignty and propounds that clarence is the vehicle from which you can see the way as well as experience the journey, safely and in comfort. It is a state and quality of being beyond balance, of being clear and certain through feeling the fractal nature of the heart.

11. Your Optimal State as defined at http://www.esencia.org.uk/index.html

12. Registered trademark re-printed here with kind permission www.heartenterprises.org.uk

13. Central to "The Esencia Model" and beautifully articulated in the song "Audition(The Fools Who Dream)", from the Original Motion Picture Soundtrack of La La Land 2016 – a firm favourite.

14. One of the NLP Magic questions – espoused in "The Way of NLP" by Joseph O'Connor and Ian McDermott, published by Thorsons on 2001. I had the privilege of attending Practitioner and Master Practitioner Programs at ITSNLP in 2004 and have incorporated these amazing techniques into my therapeutic practice ever since.

15. My professional practice www.acerelaxation.com which builds on over ten years of professional practice in effective health recovery enshrined in the Heart Enterprises® Group.

16. "Only from the heart, can you touch the sky"– Jalāl ad-Dīn Muhammad Rūmī

17. "You are not a drop in the ocean, but the entire ocean in a drop"- Jalāl ad-Dīn Muhammad Rūmī